HÄGA

T

The Conquering Hero

EGMONT/METHUEN

introducing . . .

HAGAR THE HORRIBLE
a hard-working Barbarian businessman. He's in sacking and looting.

His wife, HELGA. She finds civilizing Hagar a 24-hour-a-day job!

This is HAMLET, their son, a real problem child! He insists on wearing his hair short, bathing, reading and otherwise behaving in a very unbarbarian manner.

HONI, their daughter, is sixteen years old, and still not married!

But that's not the end of Hagar's troubles . . . there's also LUCKY EDDIE who must be the most hopeless assistant in history!

Published by Egmont Publishing Limited in association with Methuen Children's Books Limited

First Published in Great Britain 1977
Printed by William Collins Sons & Co Ltd Glasgow

ISBN 0 416 05390 4

FROM PARIS I NEED PERFUME, STOCKINGS AND SOME OF THEIR EXCELLENT LACE...
DIK BROWNE
TOO BAD YOU CAN'T GET A LITTLE CULTURE WHILE YOU'RE THERE!
©King Features Syndicate, Inc., 1973.
DON'T WORRY, BABY..... IF THEY GOT IT I'LL GET IT!
9-26

HAVEN'T YOU FORGOTTEN SOMETHING?
LEMME SEE... SHIELD, SWORD, SACK, SPEARS, AXE, MACE — NO, I THINK I REMEMBERED EVERYTHING.

OH.
© King Features Syndicate, Inc 1975 World rights reserved

YOU LOOK SILLY IN THAT HAT! WE GOTTA GET YOU A BETTER ONE...
HERE'S A PROPER HAT! TRY THIS ONE!
FORGET IT...SILLY IS BETTER THAN RIDICULOUS!

WHY DO VIKINGS WEAR HORNS, DAD?
I'LL TELL YOU IF YOU PROMISE NOT TO TELL YOUR MOTHER---
THEY'RE REALLY EAR PLUGS.

WHAT ARE YOU DOING ?
MAKING CHICKEN SOUP.
© King Features Syndicate, Inc., 1974.
2-4
THAT'S NOT THE WAY HELGA MAKES CHICKEN SOUP...
I KNOW, BUT THIS CHICKEN HAS TO LAST FOR THE WHOLE TRIP!

YOU KNOW WE GOT TWO RULES ON THIS SHIP— NO FISH AND NO WOMEN !!
©King Features Syndicate, Inc., 1974.

SORRY, DEAR— IT'S JUST NOT GOING TO WORK OUT.

DON'T WORRY, WE'LL BE HOME FOR CHRISTMAS... JUST KEEP YOUR HAND ON THE RUDDER...
12-25
AND THEN JUST FOLLOW THE STAR.
WHICH ONE ?
©King Features Syndicate, Inc., 1974.

QUICK! GET HELP!
WE'RE SINKING!

OKAY- EVERYBODY WHO WANTS TO SKIP THE GIANT'S CASTLE RAISE YOUR HAND-
5-1
1... 2... 3... 4... NO! NO!
DIK BROWNE
JUST ONE HAND, DUMMIES!
© King Features Syndicate, Inc., 1974.

WELL? DID YOU SPOT THE ENEMY?

HERE THEY COME! PREPARE TO MEET THE ENEMY!!
HOLD IT! HOLD IT!
HOW DO YOU EXPECT TO WIN WITH THAT ATTITUDE?!!

KEEP GOING, MEN! THIS IS THE ROUGH PART!
©King Features Syndicate, Inc., 1973.
THE REST IS ALL DOWNHILL!

©King Features Syndicate, Inc., 1973.
HEAR ANYTHING ?
YEAH...
SOUNDS LIKE A HUNDRED MEN MARCHING IN PERFECT STEP... HEADING RIGHT FOR US!
OH, GOOD! THEY STOPPED!

GET LUCKY EDDIE ... HE KNOWS HOW TO DO IT!
©King Features Syndicate, Inc., 1974.
WHAT MAKES HIM SO SPECIAL ?
I USED TO BE A CHICKEN PLUCKER!

BONK
BONK
SIR SWINE, HAGAR IS HERE.
SIR SWINE?
I'M SORRY, HE'S OUT.
6-7

HALT!
WHO GOES THERE? ADVANCE AND GIVE THE...

...PASSWORD

ON GUARD, KNIGHT! FIGHT, FLEE OR DIE!
© King Features Syndicate, Inc., 1973
FIRSTLY – THE CORRECT TERM IS 'EN GARDE' – SECONDLY – IT'S VULGAR TO POINT – THIRDLY – WE HAVE NOT BEEN INTRODUCED – AND LASTLY, SIR, YOU ARE UNBELIEVABLY FILTHY! GOOD DAY!
BOY! WHAT A SNOB!

HAGAR, WHO ARE WE VISITING ANYWAY?
MY BROTHER-IN-LAW

WE'VE NEVER GOTTEN ALONG VERY WELL!
DIK BROWNE
5-4
© King Features Syndicate, Inc., 1974.

DON'T WORRY— ALL HE'S GOT IS A JAB!
© King Features Syndicate, Inc., 1974.

ALL YOU GOTTA DO IS GET IN CLOSE!

DADDY WILL BE FURIOUS!
WELL, I'M SORRY... BUT I COULDN'T LEAVE ITALY WITHOUT DOING SOME SHOPPING

HI... BEEN WAITING LONG?
© King Features Syndicate, Inc., 1974.
DIK BROWNE 4-8

© King Features Syndicate Inc. 1978 World rights reserved
BUT, HAGAR — WE DON'T EVEN KNOW THESE PEOPLE...
WHAT'S THAT GOT TO DO WITH IT?

YOU DON'T THINK WE'RE BEING A LITTLE PUSHY?
11-8
DIK BROWNE

I'M LOOKING FOR ONE MAN BRAVE ENOUGH TO DEFY DEATH, SCALE THE ENEMY WALLS AND OPEN THE GATES — WHO WILL HELP ME ?!
WE ALL WILL!!
WHAT DOES HE LOOK LIKE ?
© King Features Syndicate, Inc., 1975 World rights reserved

OKAY, MEN— ACROSS THE MOAT AND UP THE LADDERS!
RIGHT!

ER... WHAT LADDERS ?
© King Features Syndicate, Inc., 1973 World rights reserved

BAM!
POK!
NOW THAT'S JUST POOR PLANNING !!
DIK BROWNE

IF YOU DON'T RETURN MY LAWN MOWER I'M GONNA KNOCK DOWN YOUR HOUSE!
HERE'S YOUR STUPID LAWN MOWER — HE DOESN'T EVEN WORK!

FOR A COLD- GIVE EXTRACT OF CIVET CAT AND HONEY.
OPEN UP, EDDIE.
BUT FIRST, SHAKE WELL.
ANYTHING YOU SAY, DOC...
© King Features Syndicate, Inc., 1975.

YOUR TROUBLE IS YOU THINK EVERYBODY IS YOUR ENEMY, THAT THE WORLD IS AGAINST YOU.
IT JUST ISN'T SO.
BUT I WOULD BUY A NEW SHIELD.

WHAT'S WRONG WITH YOUR LITTLE FINGER?

STUPID JERK! THAT'S ETIQUETTE!!

HOW'S HELGA?
NOT GOOD — SHE'S GOT THE ETIQUETTE IN HER FINGER AND IT'S DRIVING HER CRAZY!
DIK BROWNE

QUICK, HAGAR! WHERE'S THE FIRST-AID KIT?!
ON THE BOAT.
HEY, WAIT A MINUTE! WHO GOT HURT?
©King Features Syndicate, Inc., 1973.

AH! ROSE PERFUME!
DELIGHTFUL!
© King Features Syndicate, Inc., 1974.
2-13
HOW DO YOU LIKE THIS, DEAR?
TASTES ROTTEN!

AH, HAGAR! COME IN AND TAKE A SEAT.

THAT WAS A *VERY* SILLY THING TO SAY TO A VIKING.

MAKE UP YOUR MIND! IT'S EITHER ME OR YOUR BUMMY FRIENDS!
© King Features Syndicate, Inc., 1975. World rights reserved.
SORRY, DEAR.. BUT YOU DID COME IN A VERY CLOSE SECOND!

OH-OH! THAT'S BAD LUCK!
NO, NO— THAT'S JUST AN OLD WIVES' TALE
DIK BROWNE 8-14
THE HECK IT IS!
NOT WHEN IT'S MY WINE!
©King Features Syndicate, Inc., 1973.

DON'T SCUFF! PICK UP YOUR FEET!
SCUFF
SCUFF
BOOM!
ONE AT A TIME, STUPID!

LISTEN! I'M TWICE THE MAN I USED TO BE!
I GOT TWICE THE MUSCLE AND TWICE THE BRAINS!
AND THREE TIMES THE STOMACH!

IT'S A SECRET MESSAGE.
I DON'T SEE ANYTHING.
© King Features Syndicate, Inc., 1973.

NATURALLY. IT'S IN INVISIBLE INK.
WHAT DOES IT SAY?

I DON'T KNOW-- I CAN'T READ.
BOY! THAT IS A SECRET MESSAGE!

DO WE OWN A DOG?
NO, MAMA
OH, GOOD! THEN SPRING IS COMING!
© King Features Syndicate, Inc., 1974.
2-8

HAGAR IS STARTING TO SHED.
DIK BROWNE

I'M OFF TO DISCOVER THE CONTINENT OF NORTH AMERICA!
WILL YOU BE HOME FOR DINNER?
NO ONE REALLY LISTENS ANYMORE.
© King Features Syndicate, Inc., 1973 World rights reserved

I GOT THE NEW ANCHOR.
GOOD! NOW DON'T LOSE THIS ONE!
DON'T WORRY. IT'S MADE OF CORK— IT FLOATS
12-22
DIK BROWNE
© King Features Syndicate, Inc., 1975. World rights reserved.

HURRY UP! CAST OFF! GET SAILING!
I JUST HAD AN ARGUMENT WITH HELGA, AND BELIEVE IT OR NOT...
I FINALLY GOT IN THE LAST WORD!
©King Features Syndicate, Inc., 1973. World rights reserved.

IT'S GONNA BE A LONG JOURNEY TO RUSSIA!
© King Features Syndicate, Inc., 1974.
SO WHAT ?!! "A JOURNEY OF A THOUSAND MILES STARTS WITH A SINGLE STEP!" FOLLOW ME!!
BOY! IT'S GONNA BE A LONG, LONG, LONG JOURNEY!!
SPLAT!

YOU'RE NEVER HOME ANYMORE -- I HAVE TO BE THE MOTHER **AND** THE FATHER IN THIS HOUSE!
AW, YOU ALWAYS EXAGGERATE.
?
HEY, DAD, LOOK!

MY BEARD ISN'T ALL RED... THERE ARE TINY FLECKS OF SILVER AND GOLD IN IT!
DON'T YOU THINK THEY LOOK DISTINGUISHED?
THOSE ARE CODFISH FLAKES...
© King Features Syndicate, Inc., 1974.

THERE ARE ONLY TWO THINGS YOU CAN BE SURE OF—AND No.1 IS "MEN ARE SMARTER THAN WOMEN"!
CHECK
I FORGET... WHAT'S No. 2 ?
© King Features Syndicate, Inc., 1975. World rights reserved.
"THE WORLD IS FLAT"
CHECK!

I GOT A HEADACHE YOU WOULDN'T BELIEVE!
SOUNDS LIKE "THE VIKING MALADY"

WHAT'S THAT?
"INGROWN HORNS."

IF YOU DON'T LOWER YOUR STANDARDS YOU'LL NEVER GET MARRIED!
OH, MOMMA!
DIK BROWNE
7-3

AFTER ALL—YOU WOULDN'T BE HERE TODAY IF I WAS THAT PICKY!

IS YOUR MASTER GENEROUS?
HAGAR? OF COURSE.
HE'D GIVE YOU THE SHIRT OFF HIS BACK.
© King Features Syndicate, Inc., 1974.
YOU CALL THAT GENEROUS?
DIK BROWNE
6-14

WHAT'S WRONG WITH ME, DR. ZOOK?
IT IS CALLED "INSOMNIA"— THERE'S A LOT OF IT GOING AROUND.
6-20
WHAT CAN I DO FOR IT?
FIRST — GET PLENTY OF SLEEP.
DIK BROWNE
© King Features Syndicate, Inc., 1975. World rights reserved

YOU WORRIED ?
YEAH, WHAT WOULD YOU DO IF YOU WERE IN MY PLACE ?
5-10
© King Features Syndicate, Inc., 1974.
I DUNNO, BUT FRANKLY I'M WORRIED

DO I HEAR A DISTANT ROAR? THE SOUND OF GLORY? A CALL TO WAR?
©King Features Syndicate, Inc., 1973.
IT'S YOUR STOMACH.

I HAVE A MESSAGE FOR HAGAR THE HORRIBLE—HERO OF THE VIKINGS—HAVE YOU SEEN HIM?
YOU'RE LOOKING AT HIM, PAL!
1-5
DIK BROWNE

NO! I MEAN SERIOUSLY!
©King Features Syndicate, Inc., 1973.

WOW! LOOK AT THOSE CIRCLES! HOW DID YOU DO THAT ?!
ANY FOOL COULD DO THAT!
PRESENT COMPANY EXCEPTED, OF COURSE.

WHAT ARE YOU LOOKING FOR?
THE BLUEBIRD OF HAPPINESS!
IT CAN GRANT YOU ETERNAL JOY! HAVE YOU SEEN IT?
OH, GOSH...

WOW! DO YOU LOOK GREAT!
I HARDLY KNEW YOU!
BAM
S'MATTER ?! CAN'T YOU TAKE A COMPLIMENT?!

DAD, DO YOU KNOW ANY POETRY?
SURE!
A GIRL NAMED MARY HAD A WHITE LAMB THAT USED TO FOLLOW HER!
THAT'S PROSE.
HOW ABOUT THAT?! I KNOW PROSE, TOO!!

TO GET A MAN THERE ARE THREE THINGS A GIRL NEEDS.
THE FIRST IS GOOD LOOKS.
AND IF YOU GOT THAT THE OTHER TWO DON'T MATTER.

WOMEN SHOULD NOT BE TREATED LIKE BITS OF FURNITURE!
© King Features Syndicate, Inc.,
OH, WOW! THAT'S POWERFUL!
HOLD STILL WHILE I WRITE THAT DOWN!

THAT'S ENOUGH SMORGASBORD, DEAR
YOU CAN ALWAYS GO BACK FOR SECONDS

WHAT'S THAT ?
IT'S CALLED A COMPASS.
© King Features Syndicate, Inc., 1974.
WHAT DOES IT DO ?
IT SHOWS YOU HOW TO COME STRAIGHT HOME .
WHAT'S THAT ?
NOTHING !
BAM!

I GOT MY NAME ON MY SHIRT.
WHAT'S THAT?
LUCKY EDDIE
ISN'T IT ON UPSIDE DOWN?
5-8
© King Features Syndicate, Inc., 1975. World rights reserved.
NOT TO ME....
LUCKY EDDIE

YOU KNOW THE TROUBLE WITH WOMEN?
© King Features Syndicate, Inc., 1974.
THEY DON'T KNOW HOW TO RELAX AND ENJOY LIFE.
AND THAT'S ANOTHER TROUBLE ...THEY GOT ROTTEN TEMPERS!
3-16

© King Features Syndicate Inc. 1975.
WHAT IS IT?
IT'S A UNICORN.
WHAT ARE YOU GOING TO DO WITH IT?
WELL... IF I CAN GET ANOTHER ONE I'M GOING TO MAKE A HAT.

WHAT'S THAT?
"SKIS"— I JUST INVENTED THEM.

OF COURSE I DON'T HAVE ALL THE BUGS WORKED OUT.
© King Features Syndicate, Inc., 1975. World rights reserved.

WHAT A PARTY!
GIVE US A TOAST, LUCKY EDDIE!

WE WHO ARE ABOUT TO DIE SALUTE YOU!

WHY SUCH A DUMB TOAST ?!
2-18

LUCKY EDDIE! YOU KNOW WHAT I LIKE ABOUT YOU? YOU CARRY YOUR LIQUOR VERY WELL!
IN FACT, YOU'RE BETTER AT IT THAN I AM!
I SUPPOSE IT WAS MEANT AS A COMPLIMENT.
XXX

I'M NOT SAYING THAT BEING A VIKING IS FOR EVERYONE...
© King Features Syndicate, Inc., 1974.
BUT IT CAN BE A WONDERFUL BUSINESS...
IF YOU LIKE MEETING PEOPLE!
DIK BROWNE 5-18

WHERE'S LUCKY EDDIE?
I DON'T KNOW. I'VE LOOKED EVERYWHERE.

WELL, WE'LL JUST HAVE TO TEST THE NEW CATAPULT WITHOUT HIM...
zzZZZzz
© King Features Syndicate, Inc., 1975. World rights reserved.

SNEAK UP AND THROW THE TORCH OVER THE WALL, BUT BE VERY QUIET SO THE ENEMY WON'T HEAR YOU COMING!
I CAN'T PUT MY FINGER ON IT, BUT THERE'S SOMETHING WRONG WITH THIS PLAN!
7-21
© King Features Syndicate, Inc. 1975. World rights reserved.

© King Features Syndicate, Inc., 1975. World rights reserved.
THIS YOUR FIRST TIME IN SPAIN, HAGAR?
YEAH.
HOW DO YOU LIKE IT?

WELL, THE NATIVES SEEM FRIENDLY.
OLÉ!
HEY, TORO!
OLÉ!

THAT'S FUNNY- THEY DON'T ANSWER THE DOOR.

ARE YOU SURE THEY WERE EXPECTING US?

OKAY— OPEN UP AND SURRENDER!
TWAK TWAK TWAK
DOES THAT MEAN NO?
©King Features Syndicate, Inc., 1973.

WHO'LL BE FIRST TO SCALE THE WALL, DEFY DEATH AND WIN GLORY ?!
1-10
I GUESS IN A WAY THEY MEANT IT AS A COMPLIMENT
©King Features Syndicate, Inc., 1975.

BAM!
WE DID IT! WE DID IT!!
OKAY– WHAT DO WE DO NOW?
© King Features Syndicate, Inc., 1974.

HOLD THIS SEASHELL TO YOUR EAR AND LISTEN.
© King Features Syndicate, Inc. 1975 World rights reserved
IT'S FOR YOU, DAD.

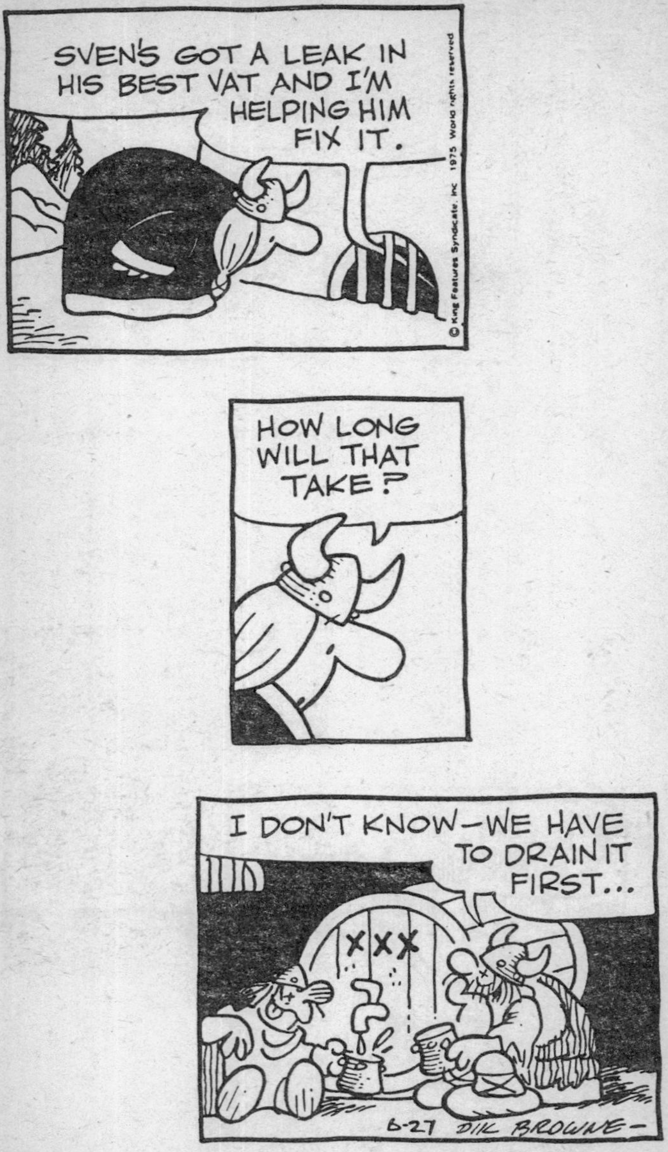
SVEN'S GOT A LEAK IN HIS BEST VAT AND I'M HELPING HIM FIX IT.
© King Features Syndicate, Inc 1975 World rights reserved
HOW LONG WILL THAT TAKE?
I DON'T KNOW—WE HAVE TO DRAIN IT FIRST...
XXX
6-27 DIK BROWNE

DID DAD REALLY PUT LONDON TO THE TORCH?
THAT'S WHAT HE TELLS PEOPLE.

MUST HAVE BEEN BEGINNER'S LUCK.

I'M COLD!
AW, STOP COMPLAINING!

©King Features Syndicate, Inc., 1973.
WHAT ARE YOU GOING TO DO WHEN WINTER COMES?

I SEE YOU GOT ONE OF THOSE SETS.
YES, BUT I WAS AGAINST IT.
AW! JUDY, JUDY, JUDY!

THERE'S NOTHING ON IT BUT KID SHOWS.
© King Features Syndicate, Inc., 1975 World rights reserved

I DON'T KNOW HOW YOU TWO CAN WATCH THAT THING.
9-5
THERE'S NOTHING ON IT BUT VIOLENCE!
POW!
TAKE THAT!
OH, YEAH?!

DAD, THE SET DOESN'T WORK.
DON'T WORRY. THAT'S EASY TO FIX.
JUST GIVE IT A KICK...
YEOW!
© King Features Syndicate, Inc. 1975 World rights reserved
9-12
DIK BROWNE

THIS ROOM IS TOO EMPTY. IT NEEDS ONE IMPORTANT PIECE OF FURNITURE.
YEAH...
©King Features Syndicate, Inc., 1973.
HOW DOES THAT LOOK?
YOU'RE A BORN DECORATOR...

WHERE ARE YOU GOING?
I DUNNO.
7-4
DIK BROWNE
DON'T GIVE ME THAT! YOU'RE GOING OUT TO DRINK WITH YOUR BUMMY FRIENDS!
OH... THAT'S RIGHT! THANKS.
© King Features Syndicate, Inc., 1975. World rights reserved.

HOW ABOUT A LITTLE SNORT?
DON'T MIND IF I DO.
HELGA SAYS IT'S UNCOUTH TO DRINK FROM THE BOTTLE.
7-5
DIK BROWNE
© King Features Syndicate, Inc., 1975. World rights reserved.

WE HAVE COME TO PREACH TO THE PAGANS.
PAGANS?
YES, PAGANS... YOU KNOW... LOST SOULS.
SOULS?
© King Features Syndicate, Inc., 1974.
OLAF! I THINK WE CAN START HERE!
DIK BROWNE 10-24

WAIT A MINUTE! A GENTLEMAN HOLDS THE DOOR OPEN FOR A LADY!
WOSH!
FUNNY, I NEVER HEARD OF THAT CUSTOM.

OKAY, OKAY– YOU CAN HAVE ONE DRINK!
DIK BROWNE
AND WHEN I SAY ONE DRINK I MEAN ONE DRINK!
BOY! YOU'D THINK I COULDN'T COUNT!

IF I'M ONE MINUTE LATE FOR DINNER SHE'LL YELL AT ME!
IF I'M REAL LATE SHE WON'T EVEN TALK TO ME!
I MUST BE NUTS! WHY AM I RUNNING?
© King Features Syndicate, Inc., 1974.
12-14
DIK BROWNE

WHAT ARE YOU DOING?
WE'RE SENDING CHRISTMAS CARDS TO OUR FRIENDS.
WE ONLY HAVE **TWO** FRIENDS?
ONLY TWO WHO CAN READ.
12-12 DIK BROWNE

HAVE A REAL VIKING DRINK!
© King Features Syndicate, Inc., 1974.
GLUG GLUG GLUG
2-7
HOW WAS IT?
IT'S OKAY...

YOU THINK WE VIKINGS DON'T DO GOOD? LOOK AT THAT VALLEY! DID YOU EVER SEE ANYTHING SO PRETTY?
© King Features Syndicate, Inc., 1974.

THAT USED TO BE A CROWDED CITY!
4-25
DIK BROWNE

STOP COMPLAINING!
KEEP GOING!

IF WE PULL THIS OFF WE'LL MAKE HISTORY!!!
© King Features Syndicate, Inc., 1973.
DIK BROWNE
10-17

YOU POOR DEVIL! THAT LOAD IS MUCH TOO HEAVY!
© King Features Syndicate, Inc., 1974.

LET ME AT LEAST LIGHTEN IT A BIT!

WHO'S PAINTING THE BOTTOM OF THE BOAT?
LUCKY EDDIE
HOW SOON WILL IT BE DRY?
TOMORROW..
...IF WE DON'T GET RAIN
© King Features Syndicate, Inc., 1974.

GIMMIE! GIMMIE! GIMMIE!
YOU WANTED HOT SOUP —I GOT YOU HOT SOUP!
10-8
DIK

NOW WHAT DO YOU WANT?!!

SOUP BOWLS!

LOOK AT THIS MAP! LOOK HOW BIG IRELAND IS!
WOW!
DID YOU KNOW IT WAS AS BIG AS EUROPE?
BIGGER!
WHERE DID YOU GET THIS MAP?
IRELAND.
© King Features Syndicate, Inc., 1975. World rights reserved

IT'S NOT FAIR! WE SPEND MONTHS LOOTING THE CAPITALS OF EUROPE AND WE COME HOME TO THIS!
RELAX!
DIK BROWNE
4-26

EVERYONE HAS TO GO THROUGH CUSTOMS!
ONE FOR YOU... ONE FOR US
© King Features Syndicate, Inc., 1974.

WON'T HELGA BE MAD?
NONSENSE! "ABSENCE MAKES THE HEART GROW FONDER."
KER-POW!
MAYBE YOU CAME HOME TOO SOON?
11-8
DIK BROWNE

© King Features Syndicate, Inc., 1975. World rights reserved.
HERE'S YOUR PILLOW – I'M GLAD WE COULD PUT YOU UP.
THANKS.
IF YOU WANT ANYTHING – JUST RING...

IT SAYS HERE: "IF YOU WOULD CONQUER THE WORLD — FIRST CONQUER YOURSELF."
© King Features Syndicate, Inc., 1975 World rights reserved
I GOTCHA!
GRUNT!
UGH!
GIVE UP?!
?

I'D LIKE THE WHALE STEAK IF IT'S FRESH.
OKAY
BUT REMEMBER— IT'S GOTTA BE FRESH!
OF COURSE
7-30
© King Features Syndicate, Inc. 1975 World rights reserved
IT'LL JUST TAKE A FEW SECONDS...

© King Features Syndicate, Inc., 1975. World rights reserved.
I THINK A FATHER SHOULD BE A PAL TO HIS SON...
NOT MY SON!
HAVE YOU SEEN HAGAR'S PALS?

ORDER FISH — IT'S BRAIN FOOD.
HOW DO YOU KNOW?
I ATE IT ALL MY LIFE.
LEMME HAVE A STEAK.
DIK BROWNE 1-22
© King Features Syndicate, Inc. 1975 World rights reserved

HEY! SVEN THE SNOB! HOW'S BUSINESS?
TRAMPLE
TRAMPLE
TRAMPLE
DIK BROWNE
THAT GOOD, HUH ?
3-24
© King Features Syndicate, Inc., 1975. World rights reserved.

I WIN! I GOT THE KING!
TOUGH! YOU LOSE. I GOT A QUEEN.
WHEN HELGA PLAYS, A QUEEN BEATS EVERYTHING.
10-10 DIK BROWNE
© King Features Syndicate Inc. 1975 World rights reserved

DIRTY DIRK, HOLD THE DOOR FOR THE LADIES.

GOD KNOWS– HE TRIES...

YOU SHOULD DO SOMETHING WITH THIS MONEY!
LIKE WHAT?
DO WHAT THE SMART PEOPLE DO. INVEST IT!! PUT IT IN LAND!
-6
WHAT DOES IT LOOK LIKE I'M DOING? I'M INVESTING!

YOU'RE GOING ON A DIET!
© King Features Syndicate, Inc., 1974.
GRRRR!
YOU, TOO!

© King Features Syndicate, Inc., 1974.
MY DAUGHTER TELLS ME YOU'RE A JESTER... JUST WHAT DO YOU DO?
TICKLE TICKLE!
PLEASE, OH, PLEASE, JUST LET HIM ASK ME WHAT I DO!!

CIVILIZING THAT HAGAR IS A 24-HOUR-A-DAY JOB!
IT IS?
DIK BROWNE 8-15

CAN YOU IMAGINE WHAT HE'D BE LIKE IF I LET UP FOR A MINUTE?!
©King Features Syndicate, Inc., 1974.

THIS SOUP IS BITTER AND COLD AND...
AND LUMPY.
© King Features Syndicate, Inc., 1974.

THE FISH JUST AREN'T BITING TODAY.
I THINK WE'VE JUST GOT THE WRONG SPOT.
8-26
DIK BROWNE
LET'S TRY OVER THERE.
© King Features Syndicate, Inc., 1974.

© King Features Syndicate, Inc., 1974.
DAD, WHY ARE YOU ALWAYS RAIDING ENGLAND?
ARE YOU KIDDING? BECAUSE IT'S FUN!
BUT IT CAN'T BE MUCH FUN FOR THE ENGLISH.
GOSH... I NEVER THOUGHT OF THAT...
WELL... I GUESS YOU CAN'T PLEASE EVERYONE!

LISTEN! I HATE TO TELL YOU TO YOUR FACE, BUT...
HOLD IT...

OKAY, GO AHEAD...
© King Features Syndicate, Inc., 1975 World rights reserved
DIK BROWNE
12-17

© King Features Syndicate, Inc., 1975. World rights reserved.
WANNA PLAY CHECKERS, DIRTY DIRK?
OKAY
BUT NO CHEATING!
ZOT!
I'LL BE DARNED! YOU WON THE FIRST GAME!
11-25 DIK BROWNE

BAM!
© King Features Syndicate, Inc., 1975 World rights reserved
BOP!
SOK!
NOW STOP THAT! THAT'S HOW FIGHTS START!
10-14
DIK BROWNE

LOOK, DR. ZOOK!
YOUR DAYS ARE NUMBERED!
IS IT A THREAT?
© King Features Syndicate, Inc., 1975. World rights reserved.
NO, IT'S A CALENDAR.

YOU'RE CRAZY!!
WELL, IF I'M CRAZY, YOU MADE ME CRAZY!
I DID NOT! YOU WERE CRAZY WHEN YOU MARRIED ME!!
I'LL DRINK TO THAT!
3-11
© King Features Syndicate, Inc., 1975. World rights reserved.

HOW DID YOU AND DAD MEET?
HE STORMED MY FATHER'S CASTLE AND CARRIED ME OFF... I WAS SO TOUCHED I MARRIED HIM. OF COURSE I WAS MUCH MORE ROMANTIC IN THOSE DAYS...
© King Features Syndicate, Inc.
AND A LOT LIGHTER.

WHAT ARE YOU DOING?
PLAYING LEAP-FROG
WHY ARE YOU SHAKING?
I'M PLAYING WITH HAGAR
DIK BROWNE
OH....
SPLAT!
© King Features Syndicate, Inc., 1974.
9-2

TAKE THE DOG FOR A WALK
AW, DO I HAVE TO?
© King Features Syndicate, Inc. 1975 World rights reserved.
LISTEN! A LITTLE WALK WON'T HURT YOU!
YEAH, BUT HE'S HEAVY!

C'MON, SNERT, ROLL OVER AND PLAY DEAD!
OKAY— THAT'S CLOSE ENOUGH...

WOW! WHAT A THROW!
OOF!
5-15
DIK BROWNE

THANKS...BUT HURRY UP WITH THAT CATAPULT... I'M GETTING TIRED...

WHAT ARE YOU DOING?
SERVING THE CREW LUNCH.
I HOPE IT'S SOMETHING NEW! THE MEN ARE SICK OF FISH BALLS!
I KNOW! I KNOW!
PONK!
BAM!
WHAK!
SPLAT!
11-21 DIK BROWNE

LOOK WHAT HAGAR GAVE US!!
WE SHOULD GIVE HIM SOMETHING NICE!
LET'S THINK — WHAT DOES HE *REALLY* LOVE?!
© King Features Syndicate, Inc., 1974.
12-17
SIGH

ACCORDING TO THIS MAP, WE'VE LEFT THE RIVER OF THE CLEAR BLUE WATER AND ARE ENTERING THE LAKE OF THE BIG SURPRISE.

WONDER WHY THEY CALLED IT THAT?
DIK BROWNE
6-16
© King Features Syndicate, Inc., 1973. World rights reserved.

I'M HUNGRY — WHAT ARE WE HAVING FOR LUNCH?
LEFTOVERS.
© King Features Syndicate, Inc., 1974.

YOU'RE LATE FOR DINNER AGAIN!

WHAT'S YOUR EXCUSE THIS TIME?!
9-9
DIK. BROWN